THE BIBLICAL MANHOOD SERIES™

WALK THRU THE BIBLE PRESENTS

PERSONAL HOLINESS
in times of TEMPTATION

LEADER'S GUIDE

DR. BRUCE H. WILKINSON

WALK THRU THE BIBLE CLASSIC

For more than three decades, Walk Thru the Bible has created discipleship materials and cultivated leadership networks that together are reaching millions of people globally through live events, print publications, audiovisual curricula, radio, television, and the Internet. Known for innovative methods and high-quality resources, we serve the whole body of Christ across denominational, cultural, and national lines. Through our strong and cooperative international partnerships, we are strategically positioned to address the church's greatest need: developing mature, committed, and spiritually reproducing believers.

Walk Thru the Bible communicates the truths of God's Word in a way that makes the Bible readily accessible to anyone. We are committed to developing user-friendly resources that are Bible-centered, of excellent quality, lifechanging for individuals, and catalytic for churches, ministries, and movements; and we are committed to maintaining our global reach through strategic partnerships while adhering to the highest levels of integrity in all we do.

Walk Thru the Bible partners with the local church worldwide to fulfill its mission, helping people "walk thru" the Bible with greater clarity and understanding. Live events and small group curricula are taught in over 50 languages by more than 60,000 people in nearly 60 countries, and more than 100 million devotionals have been packaged into daily magazines, books, and other publications that reach over five million people each year. And, in addition to our ever-expanding stock of newly created curricula, we have recently updated Walk Thru the Bible "classics" from every era of our history into digital formats. These resources, new and old, continue to bear fruit in churches, ministries, and individual lives throughout the world.

Walk Thru the Bible

Copyright 1997, 2008 © by Walk Thru the Bible. All rights reserved. Printed in the USA. *Personal Holiness* and all related products are published by Walk Thru the Bible. For more information, write: 4201 N. Peachtree Road, Atlanta, GA 30341-1362 USA, or call: (800) 763-5433. The Scripture quotations in this publication are from the New King James Version. Copyright 1979, 1980, 1982, 1990, Thomas Nelson, Inc.

PERSONAL HOLINESS
*L*EADER'S GUIDE

Table of Contents

Leading Your Group to Personal Holiness 4

Things to Remember While Leading This Series 6

Session One: *Holiness: How to Get There from Here* 8

Session Two: *Temptation: Why It's so Tempting* 10

Session Three: *Sex: A Man's Toughest Temptation* 12

Session Four: *Victory!* 14

LEADING
Your Group to Personal
HOLINESS

The Role Of The Leader

The subject of personal holiness is one of the most frequently misunderstood concepts in Christian living. And yet, the Bible speaks very clearly on the issue. The call to personal holiness is at the core of Christianity. For the serious Christian, it cannot be avoided.

As the facilitator of *Personal Holiness in Times of Temptation*, you will be leading your group into one of the most important pursuits in your spiritual journey. This *Leader's Guide* is designed to equip you for the task.

The Weapons of Warfare

Walk Thru the Bible has prepared a wealth of materials to bring the principles of this series alive in each participant's life. Your job is to guide your group through the study sessions and the exercises, allowing them to discover the concepts, embrace their meaning, and apply them to their lives.

Personal Holiness in Times of Temptation is intended to be more than just a course. It is a 30-day experience that will prepare you for the life-long process of recognizing temptation, confronting it, and neutralizing it. It contains:

Four *Video Sessions* on two DVDs, featuring the teaching of Dr. Bruce Wilkinson.

A *Course Workbook*, designed to help each participant personalize the lessons. The *Course Workbook* contains: Video Class Notes complete with a fill-in-the-blank outline for taking notes during each of the video sessions; penetrating Discussion Questions that correspond with each lesson; Daily Devotions that provide lifechanging insights for each day of the week; and Transformers, perforated Scripture and prayer cards that can be removed from the workbook, to inspire and encourage you throughout the day.

The *Discipler*, an album of four audio cassettes (one for each week) featuring the audio track of the video sessions on one side, and special, motivational challenges from Dr. Wilkinson on the other side.

Encouragers, another daily reading resource which contains personal encouragements from thirty men of God who have learned to face temptation and emerge victorious. It features special words from J.I. Packer, Chuck Colson,

Andrew Murray, Robert Munger, John White, Charles Swindoll, and more.

All of these materials can greatly enhance your experience as you study together. If you haven't already done so, take a moment to get familiar with each of these resources. (To order any of these tools for *Personal Holiness in Times of Temptation*, visit www.walkthruclassics.com.)

Getting Started—5 Easy Steps
Several basic ingredients are essential to any successful group study. Before you plan the first meeting, you should work through these fundamentals.

1. **First, pray!** Only God can change the hearts of men, and prayer is your most powerful tool. As the leader of your group, this is your logical starting place.

2. **Next, organize.** Consider asking one or two others to share the leadership load by helping you plan, promote the series, distribute materials, etc.

3. **Order the *Course Workbooks*.** Before starting the course, make sure that each participant has his own copy of the *Course Workbook*. You may want to have extra copies on hand to accommodate any late additions to your group. This series is designed to be highly interactive, and the *Course Workbook* is essential for integrating the principles into daily life.

   (If your sponsoring organization is not underwriting the cost of materials, then consider structuring your class so that the *Course Workbook* is part of a registration fee for the series.)

4. **Encourage attendance.** Walk Thru the Bible has promotional materials—such as posters and bulletin inserts—available to help you announce this series and encourage your participants to attend. (Visit www.walkthruclassics.com.)

5. **Prepare to lead the sessions.** In the following pages of this *Leader's Guide*, you will find a Session Guide for each of the four *Video Sessions*. Each one contains guidelines for the class, discussion questions, and tips. You can keep the Session Guide with you during your group time, to help you lead each session with confidence!

Things to REMEMBER While Leading This SERIES

Tried and True Tips for the Successful Video Series Leader

Cover The Material

Of all the things you do as the leader of this series, your main objective is to work through each *Video Session* and cover the discussion questions with your group in the allotted time. Each of the four video lessons is accompanied by a week's worth of devotional readings, prayers and Scriptures. There's a lot of searching and growing to be done between lessons, and it all builds on the content of the video and the discussion questions. It is **strongly recommended** that you view one, and only one, tape together each week, in order for the rest of the materials to have their full effect.

Let The Teacher Teach

For over twenty years, Dr. Wilkinson has been studying and counseling on the issue of personal holiness just so you don't have to. That means you can sit back and relax while he presents the material. Your expertise is needed in facilitating his teaching and cultivating good conversation during the discussion time. The *Leader's Guide* and the *Course Workbook* should prove helpful for your part.

Be Yourself

The others in your group will appreciate and follow your example of openness and honesty as you lead—so set a good example! The best way to encourage those in your class is not to impress them with your own holiness, but with your commitment to the pursuit of holiness. When they sense that you are "real"—that you struggle with the same issues that challenge them—they will be encouraged to press on. Someone who struggles with sin needs encouragement to overcome temptation. The transparency of your group may be the crucial ingredient that sparks their motivation.

Be Prepared

Hopefully, the discussion questions will raise some interesting conversation in your group. However, you can also lose focus during discussion time as people present opinions that may detract from the focus of the lesson, or may not represent biblical teaching. A good way to keep things on track is to point the conversation back to a related point that is covered in the *Personal Holiness in Times of Temptation* materials.

But that can only happen if you are familiar with the lessons and devotionals. Walk Thru the Bible recommends that you, as the leader, view all of the video sessions before beginning your series. Your familiarity with the series content will help you keep things headed in the desired direction at all times.

About Your Video Teacher

Dr. Bruce H. Wilkinson is your teacher for *Personal Holiness in Times of Temptation*. As the founder of Walk Thru the Bible Ministries, Dr. Wilkinson is one of America's most respected and widely appreciated Bible teachers. He has been a popular speaker at Promise Keepers Men's Conferences, where he has presented many of the principles from this series.

How To Structure Your Group Time

Whether you are leading this series in Sunday School, a men's Bible Study, or your accountability group, you'll find the materials are ideal for most small group settings. The course is designed so that the video teaching and the discussion questions will fit into an hour segment. Of course, you can take extra time for discussion or to review the previous week's material if time permits. Whatever your time frame, be sure that your group views one new video lesson per week, and that they employ the corresponding Daily Devotionals and Transformers between meetings.

The ammunition for *Personal Holiness in Times of Temptation* comes in six rounds. The first two rounds, the video session and the discussion questions, will be fired in class. The other four rounds will be fired throughout the week. Below is the suggested way to use these materials.

In Class

1. **Video Class Notes**: Each video session has a corresponding two-page spread in the *Course Workbook* for participants to follow along as Dr. Wilkinson teaches. A numbered, fill-in-the-blank outline highlights the main points of the video, and there is room for additional notes and insights as well. The "answers" to the notes can be found in each session outline of this *Leader's Guide*.

2. **Discussion Questions**: The *Course Workbook* also contains discussion questions for each of the video sessions. They are designed to help your participants personalize the content of each lesson. You can move right to these questions immediately after the conclusion of the video.

After Class

3. **Daily Devotional Readings**: These in-depth, personal studies are intended to take the principles right off the page and into the lives of each student. This is where the series moves from contemplation to application. As the participants immerse themselves in these materials each day, the transformation process begins. Urge the men in your group to read these devotionals daily. Insist on it! You may even want to include a brief review of these readings at the beginning of each week's meeting.

4. **Transformers**: Tear out the perforated Transformers cards and carry them in your pocket throughout the day. On one side is a passage of Scripture to renew your mind to holiness. The other side contains a prayer written just for the occasion. Each of the four lessons comes with three cards—one for morning, one for afternoon, and one for evening. Use the same cards each day for a week. At the end of each meeting, remind the men in your group to remove the cards for that week.
5. **Discipler**: *Discipler* is an audio album that contains the audio track of the video sessions, for review at home or in the car. Savor the points of each lesson by reviewing them daily. There's a *Discipler* for each week, and on the opposite side, you will find a special word of encouragement prepared by Dr. Wilkinson.
6. **Encouragers**: This resource contains thirty of the most rewarding articles ever compiled on the subject of personal holiness, written by thirty men of God whose lives have been transformed as they have learned to face temptation and conquer its power. There's one for each day of the month, providing a powerful supplement for this 30-day experience.

Suggested Format

1. View the Video Lesson, filling in the notes in the *Course Workbook* (25–35 minutes)

2. Review the Discussion Questions (20 minutes)

3. Clarify assignment for upcoming week (5 minutes)

4. Accountability questions, prayer requests, group prayer (10 minutes)

SESSION ONE

HOLINESS: HOW TO GET THERE *from* HERE

The Purpose Of This Session: "Holiness" has different connotations for different people. But the Bible does not waver in its definition. In order to pursue holiness with any success, you must first understand what it is. This session lays important groundwork by revealing what the Bible says about the believer's call to personal holiness.

When This Session Is Over: By the end of this session, each participant should be able to identify the three stages that make up the pursuit of Personal Holiness, and pinpoint where he is in that journey.

Video Message
Course Workbook, pages 6-7
Here are the answers for the class notes:

I. The Biblical Definition of Holiness
1. The word "holy" literally means to **separate**.
2. Holiness requires separation **from** the secular to the sacred.
3. All Christians are commanded to "be holy in all your **conduct**."

II. The Three Stages of Personal Holiness
1. The First Stage: **Salvation**—Separation unto God in God's mind.
1) The "Holy Ground" was in God's **mind**.
2) All Christians have been separated in God's mind and are **holy**.
3) The first stage of personal holiness is your salvation through trust in Christ's **sacrifice**.

2. The Second Stage: **Presentation**—Separation to God in the believer's mind
1) The "Presentation of Jesus" was in His parents' **mind**.
2) All Christians can become fully committed to **Christ**.
3) The second stage of personal holiness is your presentation of your life to God through gratitude for His love and **mercy to you**.

3. The Third Stage: **Transformation**—Separation to God in the believer's life
1) Practical holiness is a lifelong process of cleansing yourself from sin and pursuing **righteousness**.
2) Seek personal holiness "with those who call on the name of the Lord out of a pure **heart**."
3) The third stage is your transformation into the image of Christ through complete **obedience**.

Discussion
Course Workbook, page 8
How well have you understood the term "holiness"?

The Main Thing: Use the discussion questions in the *Course Workbook* to encourage the men in your group to share their thoughts. Be sensitive and allow room for specific, personal concerns to be addressed, but keep the conversation productive for the group as a whole. Now is the time to establish the trends of sticking to the lesson, dismissing on time, etc.

Additional "Conversation Starters":
What are some examples of how we can give ourselves to God as a sacrifice in this day and age?

What are some examples of things that we serve instead of God a) before salvation? b) after salvation? How are they dissimilar?

Into Action: You might suggest that the men in your group act as accountability partners for the next 30 days. You can:
1. Sign the "Holiness Commitment" form in the *Course Workbook*, and exchange phone numbers.
2. Ask each person to name a specific prayer request that the others can be praying for during the week; commit to pray for each other.

3. Ask each person to name an accountability question(s) that the group can ask him at the next meeting.

In Conclusion

Each of us is somewhere along the "Holiness Continuum." To pursue holiness, we must first understand where we are, and where we are going. The exercises in this session should "wake up" the participant to the concept of personal holiness and encourage him to commit to the process. For many men, this will be the first time they have understood that they can live in victory over sin. Remind them that victory over all temptation is God's will, and the ultimate goal of this series. The *Encouragers* resource would be a helpful motivation.

A fresh commitment to personal holiness sets the stage for our next session, which explains how to defeat sin by focusing on the temptation that precedes it.

SESSION TWO

TEMPTATION: WHY *It's so* TEMPTING

The Purpose Of This Session: Every sin a man commits is preceded by a temptation. Awareness of that fact alone should help men avoid many sins. However, there are many common misconceptions about temptation. Some say, "The Devil made me do it," while others might say, "God tempted me and I fell for it." In this session, Dr. Wilkinson dissects the relationship between temptation and sin, and exposes the common pattern that results in sin.

When This Session Is Over: After this session, the participant should be able to identify the source of his temptations, the nature of his temptations, and the limitations of his temptations. In addition, he should be able to explain two techniques to use the minute he feels tempted.

Video Message
Course Workbook, pages 22-23
Here are the answers for the class notes:

I. The Truth About Your Temptations
1. You are in dangerous territory when you think you can't **fall**.
2. Your temptations seek to **overtake you**.
3. Your temptations aren't unique to you, but are **common**.

4. God never abandons you in temptations due to His **faithfulness**.
5. God never permits any temptation to go beyond what you are **able**.
6. God always makes in every temptation the way of **escape**.
7. God always limits every temptation so that you will be able to **bear it**.

II. How Temptations Work
1. God is never the ultimate source of any evil **temptation**.
2. God is always the ultimate source of every good **gift**.
3. Every temptation purposefully seeks to **deceive**.
4. Every temptation becomes a temptation when you are **drawn away**.
5. Every temptation can only "tempt" because of your own **desires**.
6. Every temptation attempts to cunningly **entice**.
7. Every temptation has only one ultimate goal, which is your **sin**.

III. The Seven Stages of Every Temptation:
1. The **look**
2. Your **lust**
3. The **lure**
4. The **conception**
5. The **birth**
6. The **growth**
7. The **death**

Conclusion
The Quick **Signal** Principle
The Quick **Spit** Principle

Discussion
Course Workbook, page 24
Where should a man focus his effort if he is to avoid sin?

The Main Thing: The nature of these discussion questions may cause the men in your group to really open up to each other. This is good. Satan loves it when we keep our sins secret; but the personal interest, affirmation, and encouragement of the others in the group are keys to victory over temptation. However, be careful not to put an individual on the spot, forcing them to share before they're comfortable.

Additional "Conversation Starters":
What happens when we pursue external holiness without first pursuing internal holiness? Have you ever attempted this?

Imagine your strongest temptation. Do you truly believe you can ever be free from its power? What would it take to make you free?

Into Action: Encourage the men in your group to focus on identifying temptations throughout the coming week.
1. Practice identifying temptations as soon as they appear.
2. Have someone in the group describe a situation in which "The Quick Signal Principle" is used; tell the group to try it this week.
3. Now have someone describe a situation in which "The Quick Spit Principle" is used; tell the group to try it this week.
4. Ask each person their accountability question(s) from last week. Add/modify accountability questions for the next session, and renew your commitment to pray for each other.

In Conclusion
Sin is not an isolated incident, but is the result of a process which begins with

temptation. Many men are concerned about their sin, but are oblivious to the corresponding temptation.

Understanding the role of temptation is a prerequisite for doing battle with sin. The better we understand temptation, the better we can stand against it. Remind your group of the importance of the Daily Devotionals in their *Course Workbook*. This week's readings contain valuable insight about where temptations come from.

God provides a way of escape for all temptations.

SESSION THREE

SEX: A MAN'S *toughest* TEMPTATION

The Purpose Of This Session: Sexual temptations represent some of the greatest obstacles to a man's personal holiness. But God has not left us without solutions for this tension. God has not compromised His standard for holiness in this area, nor has He withheld His provision for dealing with temptation. This session is dedicated to discovering the Bible's standards regarding sexual behavior, and explaining God's provision for man's sexual needs.

When This Session Is Over: At the conclusion of this session, the participant should be able to determine which behavior in his sexual life is acceptable in God's eyes and which is not. In addition, he should be able to name the major provision God has made for his sexual fulfillment.

Video Message
Course Workbook, pages 38-39
Here are the answers for the class notes:

I. The Lord's Standards of Sexual Conduct
1. Immorality is sex before marriage with **anyone**.
2. Immorality is sex with anyone but your **wife after you are married**.
3. Immorality is any sexual activity with a man, woman, or **child** (any sexual activity other than within marriage).
4. Immorality is sexual activity with anyone or anything except your **wife**.
5. Immorality is having lustful **thoughts**.
6. Immorality is seeking anything for sexual **arousal**.
7. Immorality is looking on nakedness for **pleasure**.

II. The Lord's Provision for Sexual Temptations:

1. The primary solution to sexual immorality is sex in **marriage**.
2. The marriage partners are commanded to fulfill their sexual **duties**.
3. The body of your spouse is under your authority for your sexual **fulfillment**.
4. The request for sex is not to be denied unless both agree and for a limited **time**.
5. The postponement of sex weakens self-control and unnecessarily permits Satan to sexually **tempt**.

III. The Practical Principles of Handling Your Sex Drive.

Principle #1: **Sanctify** Yourself in Sexual Areas to be in the Will of God.
Principle #2: **Avoid** Sexual Immorality Completely.
Principle #3: **Learn** to Control Your Sexual Desires to be Holy and Honorable.
1) **Pre-commit to Abstinence**
2) **Have a Plan of Action**
3) **Have Partners in Accountability**
Principle #4: **Don't** Take Advantage of Anyone to Satisfy Your Sexual Needs.
Principle #5: **Fear** God's Discipline for All Your Sexual Immorality.
Principle #6: **Remember** God Did Not Call You to Impurity but Holiness.
Principle #7: **Depend** Upon the Holy Spirit Who Is a Gift for Your Holiness.

Conclusion:

1. The Reality of the Holy Spirit literally in your body.
2. The Responsibility to glorify God in your body.
3. The Ritual of the "Handshake of Moral and Sexual Purity."

Discussion

Course Workbook, page 40
Does God's outline for sexual behavior really result in sexual fulfillment?

The Main Thing: This discussion will bring to the surface feelings of frustration, anger, or resentment for most men, if they are honest. Your group should be a safe place where they can process these feelings openly. However, be prepared to remind the group that a healthy marriage is dependent upon many interrelated factors. This series does not attempt to address the whole picture of marital life, but only the issue of sexuality, assuming all other areas are in good order.

Additional "Conversation Starters": Chances are, not everyone in your group is married. Divide your men into three groups: married, divorced/widowed, and single men. Then ask each group to discuss the unique challenges that face them when they try to fulfill this verse in their lives:

"That every one of you should know how to possess his vessel in sanctification and honor" (1 Thessalonians 4:4).

Encourage the single men to share how they handle the added temptations of being single. What does it mean to be dishonorable when you are single? What is clearly sinful?

Into Action: Challenge the men in your group to take a step toward better communication with their wives regarding their sexual needs. This issue must be handled carefully. For some men, it

would be wise to:
1. Simply offer a humble apology for not loving his wife as he has been commanded to love her; tell her he is studying God's Word so that he may learn to love her as he is commanded to love her.
2. Ask his wife to review the track of this session (available in the *Discipler* audio album) and compare their opinions regarding the points of the lesson.
3. Conclude your discussion time by asking each person their accountability question(s) from last week. Add/modify accountability questions for the next session, and renew your commitment to pray for each other.

In Conclusion

A lack of sexual fulfillment in marriage has contributed to sexual immorality for many men, but it in no way excuses immoral behavior. Be sure your group places this lesson in the proper context with the other factors that make for a healthy marriage.

God's design includes a provision for man's sexual fulfillment. Encourage your group that God really does have our best interests in mind, if we will trust Him.

This session should encourage the participant that even in this, the toughest of man's temptations, God has answers. This sets the stage for the next session, which shows how to overcome temptation.

SESSION FOUR

VICTORY!

The Purpose Of This Session:
Tremendous personal resolve is required if a man is to overcome strong temptation and emerge victorious. However, many men are uncertain whether God even expects them to experience holiness in areas where sin currently reigns. This session reveals that it is God's will that we always succeed against temptation. It also provides an overview of the factors that determine a man's "Temptability Quotient," giving the participant heightened awareness of when he is most vulnerable.

When This Session Is Over: Upon the completion of this segment, the participant should be able to calculate his own "Temptability Quotient" and identify the "Temptation Patterns" corresponding to his greatest temptations. In addition, he should be able to name specific steps that he will take to prepare for victory in the long-term ("Holiness Habits") and in the short-term (see "IV. Victory Comes Through Turning Temptations into Triumphs!").

Video Message
Course Workbook, pages 54-55
Here are the answers for the class notes:

Introduction
1. It is the will of God that you are a man of personal holiness.
2. It is the will of God that in all temptation you experience victory.

I. Victory Comes Through Guarding Your "Temptability Quotient"
1. Physically **exhausted**/Tired
2. Emotionally **discouraged**/Down
3. Mentally **bored**/Discontent
4. Spiritually **depleted**/Empty
5. Geographically **distant**/Alone
6. Relationally **alienated**/Cold
7. Internally **hopeless**/Sad
8. Personally **insecure**/Unsure
9. Secretly **bitter**/Angry
10. Deeply **wounded**/Hurt

Scoring for "Temptability Quotient":
90–100	Great
80–89	Very Good
70–79	Careful
60–69	Danger
50–59	Extreme Danger
less than 50	Crisis

II. Victory Comes Through Breaking Your "Temptation Patterns"
1. When during your week are you tempted to sin the most?
2. What time of the day are you tempted to sin the most?
3. Where are you when you are tempted?
4. Who is nearby when you are tempted to sin the most?
5. What type of sins are you tempted to commit the most?

III. Victory Comes Through Practicing Your "Holiness Habits"
1. Scriptures
2. Supplication
3. Savior
4. Sanctification
5. Saints
6. Spirit
7. Service

Scoring for "Holiness Habits":
Column one is worth 0 points.
Column two is worth 5 points.
Column three is worth 10 points.
Column four is worth 15 points.
Column five is worth 20 points.

100+	Strong
90–100	Very Good
80–90	Good
70–80	Weak
60–70	Danger
less than 60	Extremely Weak

IV. Victory Comes Through Turning Temptations into Triumphs!
1. When tempted, run from the temptation until you reach the throne.
2. When tempted, fight back and immediately ask God to bless your pastor.
3. When most "temptable," tell Christ, your wife, and partner immediately.
4. Experience God's power, conquer your biggest sin in the next 30 days.
5. Stay tight and accountable with men who have a heart for holiness.
6. Break the back on one "temptation" by getting rid of the source.
7. Invest 30 minutes each day in your Holiness Habits.

Discussion
Course Workbook, page 56
What factors determine when you are most susceptible to temptation?

The Main Thing: In order for temptation to have any effect, we must first be temptable. Fully admitting our temptability means fully admitting our weaknesses. This is not easy for all men to do. Cultivate an atmosphere of openness and honesty about the reality of temptation's power. Remind the group that every weakness is fertile ground for Christ's strength to flourish. Determining our "Temptability Quotient" is the first step in designing our strategy to defeat temptation.

Additional "Conversation Starters":
Have you ever known someone who successfully overcame a temptation like the ones you face? If you did, how would it help you overcome your own struggles?

Why are so many men unaware of when they are most vulnerable to temptation?

Why does renewing our minds to God's word affect our behavior? Have you ever experienced this?

Into Action: Spend a few minutes sharing specific ways to apply the seven principles of "Turning Temptation Into Triumphs!" found in section IV on page 55 in the *Course Workbook*.

1. Have each person give an example of a specific situation in which one of these seven techniques might be applied in his life.
2. Have each person name a time or situation in which they are most temptable.
3. Ask each person their accountability question(s) from last week, and renew your commitment to pray for each other.

In Conclusion:
One of Satan's favorite tricks is to convince a man that his sins are a little worse than everyone else's, and a little more deplorable. Discuss this phenomenon with your group. Remind them that ALL their sins are forgiven, and that each person has the affirmation of your group, not to mention God's unconditional love.

Review the three stages of holiness described in the first session. Ask each group member to give a brief update on where they are in "The Practical Process of Personal Holiness" chart on page 7 in the *Course Workbook*. Have they made any progress compared to where they were at the start of this series?